Troubleshooting Search in SharePoint Online

Mikael Svenson

Table of contents

Introduction   5

1 Prerequisites and audience   6

  PnP PowerShell   7

  Crawl Log Permission   8

  Search with elevated privileges   10

2 Tools   12

  SharePoint Search Query Tool   12

  Get-PnPSearchCrawlLog   16

  Submit-PnPSearchQuery   18

  Get-PnPSearchConfiguration   19

3 Search schema, crawled properties, managed
properties and the full-text index   20

  Crawled properties   21

  Managed properties   23

  Automatically created managed properties   24

  Full-text index   29

  Rank profile   29

  Querying using managed properties   30

  What makes a SharePoint column searchable?   32

  Search schema mapping levels   35

  Searching for and retrieving managed properties   37

4 Troubleshooting scenarios   39

  User has access to the item, but the item is not
    showing in search   40

  The search result item does not reflect the
    SharePoint item   48

Troubleshooting steps   50

    Crawled and managed properties issues   64

    Searching against managed metadata   77

    Impact of query language in search   79

    Duplicate instances of refiner values   80

    Why does one item appear above another in
       the search results?   81

    API issues causing partial results being returned   85

5 Re-index the list, library or site   87

    Re-indexing a list or library   87

6 Re-index user profiles   89

7 Query modifications   91

    Check if a query was modified   91

    Browser debug   93

    SharePoint Search Query Tool debugging   94

8 External users and search   95

9 Interpreting crawl log errors   96

    Parser: Document was partially processed. The
       parser was not able to parse the entire document.   96

    Parser: Max output size of 2000000 has been reached
       while parsing!   96

10 File a support ticket   97

11 Community information   98

Introduction

Over the years I have many a time assisted myself and others in solving seemingly hard search challenges. Often it boils down to figuring out or knowing how search in SharePoint and SharePoint Online works behind the scenes. Other times there are actual bugs or degradations in the search service and being able to surface as much information as possible when filing a support tickets ensures a quicker resolution.

In this book I will cover the tools I use to figure out what is going on and explain the steps you can take when you encounter search issues you need to figure out.

The content of this book is a brain dump of information I have accumulated over the years. Some is self-experienced, some is inspired by the community and colleagues, and some of it from the official documentation at **docs.microsoft.com**[1].

I'll call out Waldek, Trevor, Agnes, Matt, Dan Göran and Ole Kristian specifically as they have been my search buddies for a good long while. Others have also contributed and inspired much of the content, and if you feel you helped contribute to the contents of this book, a big thank you! It would not have been possible without the very vibrant community which the SharePoint community truly is.

Sharing is caring!

May the Search be with you! – Mikael Svenson

---

[1] https://docs.microsoft.com/sharepoint

1 Prerequisites and audience

The focus of this book is mainly figuring out why search results are not what you expect them to be, focusing on the discoverability of content and not on how to craft smart search queries for specific solutions and scenarios.

The primary audience for this book is IT administrators, SharePoint developers and SharePoint consultants. If you are a power-user or citizen developer you should also find the book useful, depending on your technical skillset and understanding of SharePoint.

Having a rudimentary technical understanding of SharePoint in general and what SharePoint search is will make it easier to follow the concepts shown in this book as some of the material require background knowledge.

This book does not cover troubleshooting of hybrid search specific scenarios.

You can find a lot of introductory content to get you started at **Search in SharePoint in docs.microsoft.com**[2].

---

[2] https://docs.microsoft.com/sharepoint/dev/general-development/search-in-sharepoint

PnP PowerShell

When working with administration, configuration and development in SharePoint Online using Patterns and Practices (PnP) PowerShell cmdlets should be second nature.

Being a core member of the PnP team, I have contributed several cmdlets to help with search in SharePoint Online.

Submit-PnPSearchQuery	Executes an arbitrary search query against the SharePoint search index
Get-PnPSearchCrawlLog	Returned crawl information for indexed items
Get-PnPSearchConfiguration Set-PnPSearchConfiguration	Work with the classic search configuration and schema for the given scope/site
Get-PnPSearchSettings Set-PnPSearchSettings	Configure search page behavior on a site

See the **official documentation**[3] on how to install PnP PowerShell, and the **cmdlet technical reference**[4] for detailed cmdlet descriptions and documentation.

---

[3] PnP PowerShell Overview https://docs.microsoft.com/powershell/sharepoint/sharepoint-pnp/sharepoint-pnp-cmdlets

[4] SharePoint PnP PowerShell - https://docs.microsoft.com/powershell/module/sharepoint-pnp

Crawl Log Permission

To access crawl log entries from the SharePoint Online crawl log, you first need to grant the user permissions directly or via a security group.

Perform the following steps to grant permissions to view crawl log information:

1. Sign in to *https://admin.microsoft.com* as a global or SharePoint admin. (If you see a message that you don't have permission to access the page, you don't have the necessary Office 365 administrator permissions in your organization.)

2. In the left pane, under **Admin centers**, select **SharePoint**. (You might need to select **Show all** to see the list of admin centers.) If the classic SharePoint admin center appears, select **Open it now** at the top of the page to open the new SharePoint admin center.

3. Choose **Classic features**.

4. Under **Search**, select **Open**.

5. On the search administration page, choose **Crawl Log Permissions**.

6. In the **Crawl Log Permissions** box, enter names or email addresses. The names of valid users or user groups are shown in the list as you type letters in the box.

7. Select **OK**.

Once these steps are completed you should be able view crawl log information using the **Get-PnPSearchCrawlLog** cmdlet.

Search with elevated privileges

There are scenarios where you need to elevate the context when performing search operations in the same manner as eDiscovery in Office 365 does.

> *Beware of elevating permissions in a tenant as anyone who can access the elevated credentials will be able to search all content indexed, possibly breaching security and privacy regulations and laws.*

To elevate search privileges, connect to SharePoint Online using app-only permissions. You can either use the classic SharePoint app-only model, or you can configure app-only via an Azure Active Directory Application registration (ADAL).

For the SharePoint app-only approach you need to set tenant *FullControl* permissions. See the Granting access using **SharePoint App-Only for how to set this up**[5].

If you however are using an ADAL application, you need to at the minimum add *Sites.Read.All* permissions to your application in order to elevate.

---

[5] https://docs.microsoft.com/en-us/sharepoint/dev/solution-guidance/security-apponly-azureacs

For help on configuring an ADAL application with certificates and SharePoint API access, see the sample **Connect to the SharePoint Online using Application Permissions**[6] at the PnP PowerShell GitHub repo.

---

[6] https://github.com/SharePoint/PnP-PowerShell/tree/master/Samples/SharePoint.ConnectUsingAppPermissions

2 Tools

To help assist troubleshooting search results in SharePoint
Online there are two main sources of information: the search
results themselves and the crawl log.

The crawl log will yield information on the ingestion of items
to the search index and if there were any errors or warnings
during indexing. Searching for items is of course what it is all
about to see if they are returned in the way you expect.

Seems simple right?

Turns out it's harder than one might expect, and you must
arm yourself with a set of community tools built for this exact
purpose of troubleshooting.

SharePoint Search Query Tool

The SharePoint Search Query Tool is the tool I by far use most
often, and which I happen to be the maintainer of.

The first version was released back in 2012 to support
SharePoint 2013, and has since been modified and adapted
with new releases coming at irregular intervals.

The application is a Windows application primarily used to
test out different search queries and query parameters and
used to inspect the raw data being returned. It might lack
detailed documentation, but every property or toggle in the
tool maps to a search API setting.

The minimum settings you should acquaint yourself with are
as follows.

Query Text	To mimic text entered by a user
Trim Duplicates	To turn off duplicate trimming
Select Properties	Comma separated list of the managed properties you want to return values for.
Refiners	Comma separated list of the refinable managed properties you want to see refiner values for.
Result Source Id	Can usually be left blank, and you will then use the default result source on the end point you log into.

For people search, change this to "Local People Results". |
| Query Template | In case you want to test query variables as part of your query. |

The SharePoint Search Query Tool can be downloaded from the **PnP Tool GitHub repository**[7].

---

[7] https://github.com/SharePoint/PnP-Tools/releases

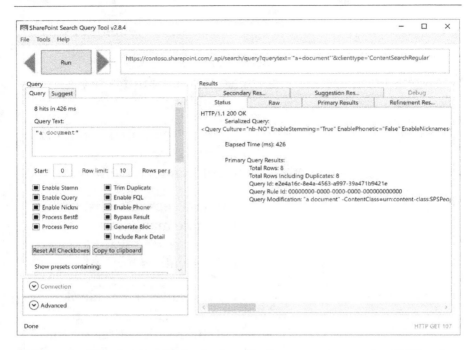

When connecting to SharePoint Online you enter the URL of the site collection you want to run queries against in the connection settings. You can use the root site collection URL for your tenant https://<tenant>.sharepoint.com or any other site, but the URL will matter if you have:

- Changed the default result source on a site collection.
- Added a query rule on a site collection.

If you work with one tenant only it's safe to use **SharePoint Online (Web login)** as the login method. If you work with multiple tenants, you want to pick the **SharePoint Online (App Id)** login option to get the least amount of connection problems. If you have TMG/UAG or custom ADFS configured, you might want to try one of the login methods.

⌃ Connection

SharePoint Site URL: https://contoso.sharepoint.com

Timeout (sec): 30

Accept: ● json ○ xml

Method: ● HTTP GET ○ HTTP POST

Authentication: Authenticate using specific user account ⌄

Authentication Method: SharePoint Online (App Id) ⌄

Sign-in

SharePoint Online (Web login) will also work, but for a domain joined PC, you will find it difficult to connect to any other tenant outside of the one you are logged into.

Get-PnPSearchCrawlLog

The crawl log tracks information about the status of crawled content. This log lets you determine whether crawled content was successfully added to the index, or whether indexing failed because of an error. The crawl log also contains information such as the time of the last successful crawl and the last modified time of the item. Having access to this information is often a good starting point to diagnose problems with the search experience.

Contrary to SharePoint on-premises, SharePoint Online does not have a separate built-in UI to examine the search crawl log. However, you can get to the information programmatically via the CSOM API which is what the cmdlet **Get-PnPSearchCrawlLog** in PnP PowerShell uses.

> *It is possible to access the crawl log via the user interface in the eDiscovery portal, but I find using PnP PowerShell more convenient for troubleshooting scenarios.*

To list crawl log entries for a document stored at the URL `https://contoso.sharepoint.com/teams/MyTeam/Shared Documents/A document.docx` first connect to a SharePoint site you have access to (any site or admin site will do), and then filter out results for that document only:

```
Connect-PnPOnline -Url
https://contoso.sharepoint.com/teams/MyTeam

Get-PnPSearchCrawlLog -Filter "
https://contoso.sharepoint.com/teams/MyTeam/Shared
Documents/A document.docx"
```

The result will look similar to the below output, displaying the last crawl entry for the file. *CrawlTime* is in UTC date format, while *ItemTime* is relative to the time zone of the site the item is stored at. For the below output, the site's time zone was set to PST, a difference of 7 hours from UTC. You also see the item was crawled 10 seconds after the document was saved, which means indexing was almost instant.

```
Url             :
https://contoso.sharepoint.com/teams/MyTeam/Shared
Documents/A document.docx
CrawlTime       : 14.07.2019 14:05:32
ItemTime        : 14.07.2019 21:05:16
LogLevel        : Success
Status          :
ItemId          : 7062366
ContentSourceId : 1
```

If you want to look at the raw unparsed data coming from the crawl log, use the **-RawFormat** switch when issuing **Get-PnPSearchCrawlLog**. The *RawFormat* switch will also yield information showing if the item was excluded for some reason or if it was deleted.

Submit-PnPSearchQuery

The easiest approach to return a specific item from the search index is to use a property filter on the managed property **path**.

To list crawl log entries for a document stored at the URL `https://contoso.sharepoint.com/teams/MyTeam/Shared Documents/A document.docx` first connect to a SharePoint site you have access to (any site or admin site will do), and then filter for that document only:

```
Connect-PnPOnline -Url
https://contoso.sharepoint.com/teams/MyTeam

Submit-PnPSearchQuery -Query 'path:"
https://contoso.sharepoint.com/teams/MyTeam/Shared
Documents/A document.docx"' -RelevantResults
```

The result output is one item with all the default managed properties returned.

```
Rank              : 16,072546005249

WorkId            : 17640090084906

Title             : A document

Author            : Mikael Svenson

Size              : 18637

Path              :
https://contoso.sharepoint.com/teams/MyTeam/Shared
Documents/A document.docx

Write             : 14.07.2019 14:09:20

LastModifiedTime  : 14.07.2019 14:09:20

...etc.
```

Get-PnPSearchConfiguration

This cmdlet allows you to get the XML configuration for a site, site collection or the tenant listing any change to search configuration at that scope.

The XML contains the setup of crawled to managed property mappings, result source configurations, result type configurations, and query rule definitions including best bets.

Reading the output XML is not easy, but the cmdlet has a special mode to list all the crawled to managed property mappings, which is typically what you need to look at.

To list the tenant wide crawled property to managed property mappings you run the following commands:

```
# Connect to the admin site
Connect-PnPOnline -Url https://contoso-
admin.sharepoint.com
Get-PnPSearchConfiguration -Scope Subscription -
OutputFormat ManagedPropertyMappings
```

The result output will list all the manually mapped crawled properties to managed properties globally for your tenant.

```
PS> Get-PnPSearchConfiguration -Scope Subscription -OutputFormat ManagedPropertyMappings

Name                        Aliases            Mappings                                                                    Type
----                        -------            --------                                                                    ----
DiscoveryDomainFilterOWSTEXT {}                {ows_q_TEXT_DiscoveryDomainFilter}                                          Text
FullHTMLOWSHTML             {}                 {ows_r_HTML_FullHTML}                                                       Text
HideFromDelve               {}                 {ows_HideFromDelve}                                                         YesNo
HideFromSearch              {}                 {ows_HideFromSearch}                                                        YesNo
ipbody                      {}                 {ows_ipbody}                                                                Text
iptitle                     {}                 {ows_iptitle}                                                               Text
mAdcOWText                  {}                 {ows_q_URLH_mAdcOWUrl}                                                       Text
NoRecall                    {}                 {11, 9, 2}                                                                  Text
owstaxIdmadcowRegion        {}                 {ows_taxId_madcowRegion}                                                    Text
RichTextOWSMTXT             {}                 {ows_r_MTXT_RichText}                                                       Text
TagBoost                    {}                 {ows_taxId_MetadataAllTagsInfo}                                             Text
RefinableString00           {}                 {ows_refvalue, ows_RefRoot}                                                 Text
RefinableString03           {multivaluetest}   {ows_Multivalie}                                                           Text
RefinableString06           {}                 {ows__UIVersionString}                                                      Text
RefinableString07           {}                 {ows__ModerationStatus}                                                     Text
RefinableString05           {MultiValueSemiSep} {ows_MultiString2}                                                        Text
2                           {}                 {Title, TermTitle, 2, ows_BaseName...}
RefinableString04           {MultiValueSPSep}  {ows_MultiString}                                                          Text
RefinableDate01             {}                 {LastModifiedTime}                                                          Date
RefinableDate00             {}                 {ows_Modified}                                                              Date
Date00                      {}                 {urn:schemas-microsoft-com:sharepoint:portal:profile:SPS-Birthday}          Date
RefinableInt00              {}                 {ows_refvalue}                                                              Integer
```

3 Search schema, crawled properties, managed properties and the full-text index

When content is indexed into the search index, that content is represented via a search schema. In SharePoint Online the search schema from a content perspective consists of:

- Crawled properties, one for each entity of metadata related to the content being indexed.
- Managed properties, being mapped to one or more crawled properties, adding behavior to the metadata such as allowing it to be retrieved as part of a search result, or allowing to filter or sort the search results on the metadata.
- Two full-text indexes, one for user profile content and one for all other content. When a user issues a free form query like *"sharepoint online search"*, the terms will be matched against the full-text index, consisting of all searchable content from documents and items.
- Rank profiles which defines how content in the full-text index and managed properties should be treated from a rank perspective. For example, term match in a title is more important compared to a term match on page 25 in a document.

Crawled properties

A crawled property consists of content and metadata extracted from an item, such as a document or a list item during a crawl – in short, any content metadata that has entered SharePoint search during content crawling or that has been extracted in the indexing pipeline.

As an example, a crawled property can be an author, the title of the item, or the subject of an e-mail. When you create either a list or a site column in SharePoint, a crawled property will be created matching the column once you add an item which populates the column with data.

Say you create a column named *Foo*. Once an item is added to SharePoint with a value set in this column a crawled property named *ows_Foo* will be created in the search schema for this column. The prefix ows stems from the original code name for SharePoint – Office Server, and stands for Office Web Server. Sometimes pieces of legacy sticks with us for backwards compatibility and historical reasons.

If multiple places in SharePoint have named a column with the same name, the same crawled property will be used for all of them – regardless of the column type.

If a custom column is used for a document library, then an additional crawled property with the column is added if used in Office type documents, as the column and value is embedded in the file itself, and will be extracted as part of the document parsing process. The value for the crawled properties *Foo* and *ows_Foo* in the above case should be the same.

Related to the above, any file format with custom properties in them, which is parsed during indexing, will receive a crawled property which may be used in search, regardless if there is a corresponding column for it or not.

By default, the content from inside a document as well as content from a crawled property (metadata) will be *searchable*. Searchable means that when a free-text query is performed, it will match content from these crawled properties, which are all stored in the full-text index.

Managed properties

Managed properties are used to represent one or more crawled property in the search index. After mapping managed properties from crawled properties, you can use managed properties to construct targeted queries, use them for sorting, use them as refiners, or use them to retrieve values back in the search result.

Managed properties also have a data type which allows different kinds of queries:

- Text
- Integer
- Decimal
- Date and Time
- Yes/No
- Double precision floating
- Binary

In addition, you can set other characteristics for managed properties, where many only apply to the text types.

See **Managed property setting overview**[8] in the official documentation for a thorough explanation of the different settings.

---

[8] https://docs.microsoft.com/en-us/sharepoint/search/search-schema-overview#managed-property-settings-overview

Automatically created managed properties

To complicate matters even more, SharePoint has a concept of **Automatically or implicitly created managed properties**. When you in SharePoint create a site column and use that column in a list or library, instead of just getting one crawled property, you will get two crawled properties and one managed property – which is mapped to one of the crawled properties.

If you are an admin or developer setting up columns in SharePoint, I highly recommend using site columns over list columns for ease of use and management.

Mikael's managed property rule of four

Never ever mess with the out of the box managed properties.

Use automatic/implicit managed properties if possible.

Map crawled properties to the RefinableXXYY re-usable properties if possible, with an identifiable alias for easier management and use.

Create a custom managed property as a last resort with a good identifiable prefix or alias.

The default settings for an automatic managed property (has capital letters OWS in the name) are:

- Queryable
- Retrievable
- Multi-value (taxonomy and multi-user columns only)
- Searchable (taxonomy columns only)
- **Always of type text!**

If you need different behavior from a managed property, for example making it refinable, or perform a property query for a number or a date, then visit the rule of four above.

Official documentation for automatic managed properties can be found at **Automatically created managed properties in SharePoint Server**[9].

As mentioned earlier the default naming for a crawled property is *ows_columnName*.

---

[9] https://docs.microsoft.com/sharepoint/technical-reference/automatically-created-managed-properties-in-sharepoint

The naming convention for the automatically created crawled and managed property pairs can be seen in the table below, and these are in addition to the *ows_columnName* crawled property.

Site column type	Crawled property name	Managed property name
Single line of text	ows_q_TEXT_Site ColumnName	SiteColumnNa meOWSTEXT
Multiple lines of text	ows_r_MTXT_Sit eColumnName	SiteColumnNa meOWSMTXT
Choice	ows_q_CHCS_Sit eColumnName	SiteColumnNa meOWSCHCS
Choice (allow multiple selections)	ows_q_CHCM_Si teColumnName	SiteColumnNa meOWSCHCM
Number	ows_q_NMBR_Sit eColumnName	SiteColumnNa meOWSNMBR
Currency	ows_q_CURR_Sit eColumnName	SiteColumnNa meOWSCURR

Site column type	Crawled property name	Managed property name
Date and Time	ows_q_DATE_SiteColumnName	SiteColumnNameOWSDATE
Yes/No	ows_q_BOOL_SiteColumnName	SiteColumnNameOWSBOOL
Person or Group	ows_q_USER_SiteColumnName	SiteColumnNameOWSUSER
Hyperlink or Picture	ows_q_URLH_SiteColumnName	SiteColumnNameOWSURHL
Publishing HTML	ows_r_HTML_SiteColumnName	SiteColumnNameOWSHTML
Publishing Image	ows_q_IMGE_SiteColumnName	SiteColumnNameOWSIMGE
Publishing Link	ows_q_LINK_SiteColumnName	SiteColumnNameOWSLINK
Managed	ows_taxId_SiteCo	owstaxIdSiteCo

Site column type	Crawled property name	Managed property name
Metadata	lumnName	lumnName
Integer*	ows_q_INTG_Site ColumnName	SiteColumnNa meOWSINTG
GUID*	ows_q_GUID_Sit eColumnName	SiteColumnNa meOWSGUID
Grid Choice*	ows_q_CHCG_Sit eColumnName	SiteColumnNa meOWSCHCG
ContentTypeI DFieldType*	ows_q_CTID_Site ColumnName	SiteColumnNa meOWSCTID
SPS average rating	ows_q_RAVG_Sit eColumnName	SiteColumnNa meOWSRAVG
SPS rating count	ows_q_RCNT_Sit eColumnName	SiteColumnNa meOWSRCNT

Full-text index

A full-text index is a property containing many managed properties. A full-text index is what SharePoint search uses behind the scenes when you run an untargeted query. Just like you can map crawled properties into managed properties, you define a full-text index by mapping managed properties into it. You also set different levels of importance on each managed property that you map into a full-text index. These levels are used when SharePoint search is calculating a given item's relevance against a certain search query.

Rank profile

The last key concept of the index schema is the rank profile. A rank profile is referenced by a full-text index and defines more specifically how the different managed properties in the full-text index should contribute to rank calculations. For SharePoint on-premises you can define these profiles yourself, but in SharePoint Online these are provided for you by Microsoft, employing machine learning to adapt best to the content indexed and search use-patterns.

Querying using managed properties

The other way of searching is by issuing a property query. Property queries are targeting values in managed properties.

The below query will yield results where the managed property author contains the name "Mikael Svenson".

```
author:"Mikael Svenson"
```

The value for the managed property author again comes from one or more crawled properties, metadata on the indexed item. Below is a screenshot of the default mappings found in my test tenant. Deciphering what the crawled properties mean can be hard but for most SharePoint items a column will translate to a crawled property named *ows_<column name>*.

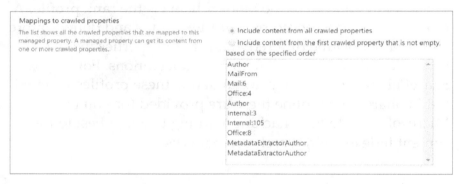

Managed properties can have many settings, or attributes. These attributes determine how the contents are shown in search results. The search schema contains the attributes on managed properties and the mapping between crawled properties and managed properties.

To learn more about SharePoint Search and search queries, check by book **SharePoint Search Queries Explained**[10].

[10] https://www.amazon.com/dp/B00RO84UBQ

To learn more about crawled and managed properties in SharePoint Online, read the official documentation **Overview of crawled and managed properties in SharePoint Server**[11].

It's also beneficial to read **Manage the search schema in SharePoint Server**[12] which explains how you map a crawled property to a managed property.

---

[11] https://docs.microsoft.com/sharepoint/technical-reference/crawled-and-managed-properties-overview

[12] https://docs.microsoft.com/sharepoint/search/manage-the-search-schema

What makes a SharePoint column searchable?

By searchable I mean a user searches for a term and get a search result back if that term exists in a SharePoint column (without specifying a property query). Basically, typing keywords in a search box.

By default, when you create a SharePoint column on a list, a crawled property is generated which is marked with **Include in full-text index**. This checkmark ensures you will get a hit for terms in this column. The naming of the crawled property is **ows_internalColumnName**. In SharePoint Online it is not possible to change this behavior.

If you look at managed properties, they have a corresponding property called **Searchable**. This means if your crawled property is mapped to a managed property marked as searchable, search results are returned when search terms match content in this column. However, if the managed property is not marked as searchable, even though the crawled property is marked with **Include in full-text** index, it will NOT be searchable.

To put it all in a table which reads per row for how a SharePoint column relates to a crawled and managed property mapping, and the full-text index settings per property.

Crawled Property		Managed Property		SharePoint
Included in Full text-index	Not included in Full text-index	Searchable	Not Searchable	Column Searchable
x				✓
	x			✗
x		x		✓
	x	x		✓
x			x	✗
	x		x	✗

If a crawled property is mapped to two or more managed properties, where one of them is searchable, then the value will be searchable.

If a SharePoint column is set to be hidden or marked via column properties as **NoCrawl**, then the column will not be searchable.

Below is a sample PnP PowerShell script to check and/or change settings for a list column. The same can be used on site columns as well by omitting the *List* parameter.

```
# Connect to the site
Connect-PnPOnline
https://contoso.sharepoint.com/sites/mysite

# Load the title field for a document library
$field = Get-PnPField -List Documents -Identity Title -
Includes NoCrawl,Hidden

# Output existing values
$field.NoCrawl
$field.Hidden

# Change values
$field.NoCrawl = $false
$field.Hidden = $false

# Save changes
$field.Update()
Invoke-PnPQuery
```

If the crawled property is from a number/currency column, you need to map it to a searchable managed property to get full-text index matches.

To sum it all up.

In order to make a column in SharePoint NOT be searchable, you either have to uncheck the option on the corresponding crawled property to include it in the full-text index (not available for SharePoint Online), or map it to a managed property which is not marked as searchable.

Search schema mapping levels

In SharePoint search you can map a crawled property to a managed property at two different levels: Tenant level (subscription) and site collection level.

For ease of use and maintenance, always map at the tenant level if you can. This makes troubleshooting a lot easier.

If you really know what you are doing and you are creating a search solution hosted and visible in one site only, then mapping at the site collection level makes sense – but be sure to document it.

Tenant level

The tenant level is the top-level search schema level for your tenant and applies to all the content stored in SharePoint. Tenant level administration can be found via search administration in the SharePoint admin center.

Mappings at the tenant level are inherited down to all site collections and sub sites.

Mappings for content outside of a SharePoint site collection like user profiles and hybrid crawled data, **must** be mapped at the tenant level.

Site collection level

Mappings at a specific site collection will have effect for content stored on that site collection only. This means the managed property will get populated with data from the crawled properties mapped at that one site collection. If the managed property has mappings at the tenant level as well, those are overwritten with by the site collection level schema mappings.

All mappings for a site collection are also inherited down to any sub sites.

As an example. If an item's *Title* managed property has been remapped on a site collection to contain the value of the column *MyBetterTitle*, using *ows_BetterTitle*, then search results with those items will have *BetterTitle* returned.

Read more at **https://docs.microsoft.com/sharepoint/manage-search-schema** and **https://docs.microsoft.com/SharePoint/search/manage-the-search-schema**.

Searching for and retrieving managed properties

When SharePoint 2013 first came out, managed property names were case insensitive. For a site column of type number named *MyFoo* you will get an automatic managed property named *MyFooOWSNMBR*. If you queried or retrieved this managed property by typing:

myfooowsnmbr instead of *MyFooOWSNMBR*, the result would be the same.

However, in SharePoint Online you must use the correct casing as managed property names are case sensitive. This change was made for performance reasons to achieve cloud scale.

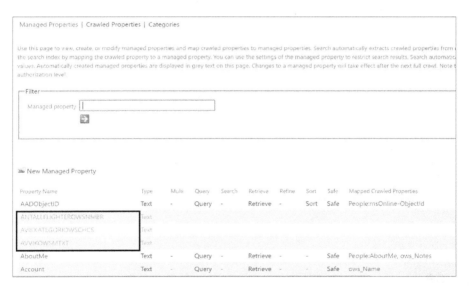

To ensure you are using the correct casing search for a managed property in the schema admin UI and copy the exact casing you see there.

Casing applies specifically to the managed properties in the color grey, but I recommend using the correct casing for all managed properties to avoid any potential issues.

4 Troubleshooting scenarios

At a high level the four most common troubleshooting scenarios with search in SharePoint Online are:

- The item is not showing in the search results
- The item shown in search is not the same as the item stored in SharePoint
- The item is not being returned using text known in the document/list item
- Why is the item shown as number X in the results?

Troubleshooting the first three scenarios are almost identical. The fourth scenario however can be tricky to figure out and requires a deeper understanding of SharePoint search and will be covered separately.

Before you start to troubleshoot it helps to understand the most common reasons why an item is not appearing as expected in the search results and I want to state that there are no guarantees in SharePoint Online on how quick and item is indexed after it is updated.

Any time interval mentioned is therefore best effort approximations based on personal observations. So, when I state items are updated usually within 5 minutes, you could see both 6 hours and 24 hours if the farm hosting your tenant is experiencing issues or a very heavy load for some reason.

User has access to the item, but the item is not showing in search

A common troubleshooting scenario is when a user reports he/she can view the item fine in SharePoint, but it's not appearing in the search results. This is usually caused by a permission issue or the item not being in the index at all.

Permissions are out of synch

When a SharePoint item is indexed, the access control lists (ACLs) on who has read access to the item is also included in the search index. This ensures that if you can read an item in SharePoint, you should also be able to see the item as a search result.

There are however scenarios where the ACLs are not identical in the search index and in SharePoint.

If the user trying to find an item has been granted access to the item via direct access after the item was first indexed, then the item has to be re-crawled in order for the search index to know that a new user should have access to the item.

This will be the case when an item or site has been shared with an external user.

Direct access means permission is granted to the user via sharing of the item, folder, library or site, or the user being added to a SharePoint security group.

If a user is granted permission by being added to an Office 365 Group or an Azure Active Directory security group, then the user should get almost immediate access to the item via search.

For any change to an item itself, re-indexing happens usually within 5 minutes. When security changes, this is picked up by security crawls, which runs on longer intervals. You should still expect to see security changes being picked up quickly.

If you do not see security changes being picked up within an hour, you can try to trigger a list, library or site to be queued up for re-indexing. There is however no guarantee that this will speed up the indexing, but rather will have a taxing effect on the overall crawl system for Office 365 as items may be crawled twice.

Item does not have a major version

In SharePoint Online only major versions of items are being indexed. For lists and libraries which have major and minor versioning enabled, you must ensure *Draft Item Security* is set to *Any user who can read items,* in order for the item to be indexed and searchable as the draft version.

If set to another value only published major versions will be indexed and made searchable. Publishing a major version is a manual step. For documents and items, you can find the option via ellipses menu for the document.

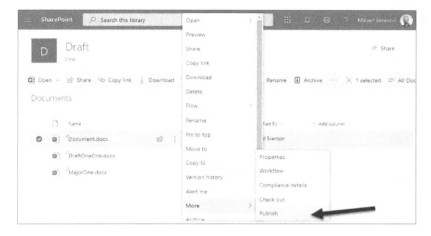

For a modern page, click the *Publish* button to create a major version.

Once a major version is published, the item will be indexed and made searchable.

See **Enable and configure versioning for a list or library**[13] on how to change the version settings for a list or library in SharePoint.

---

[13] https://support.office.com/article/enable-and-configure-versioning-for-a-list-or-library-1555d642-23ee-446a-990a-bcab618c7a37

List, library or site has been set to not being indexed

Both lists/libraries and sites in SharePoint can be set not to be indexed by search. If this is the case, then items will not appear in search results.

For lists and libraries this setting can be found under *Advanced settings*.

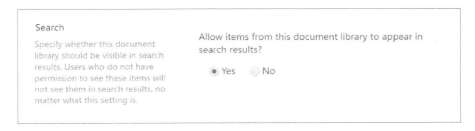

For a site, the setting is located under Search and Offline Availability (`https://<tenant>.sharepoint.com/sites/yoursite/_layouts/15/ srchvis.aspx`).

If the indexing was turned off, you need to re-index the items for the items to appear in your search results.

Duplicate trimming

Depending on the search UI you are using in classic or modern, the search results may be subjected to trimming away duplicates. SharePoint uses a technique to trim on near duplicates where four checksums are generated based on metadata for the item, and if one of these matches with another item, only one of the items will show.

By default, duplicate trimming is **turned on** in the search API, so it's up to the application or web part to turn it off.

For classic search web parts, you find the setting on the *Settings* tab in the query builder.

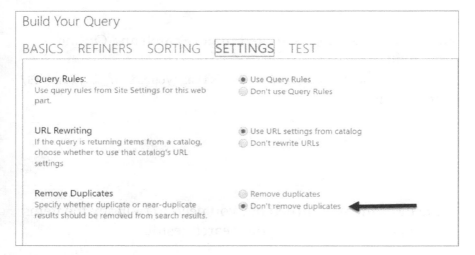

In the SharePoint Search Query Tool, you turn off duplicate trimming by unchecking the *Trim Duplicate* setting.

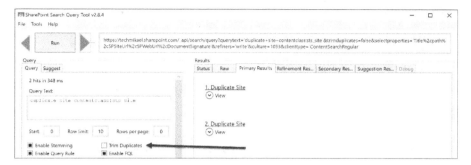

PnP PowerShell cmdlets and the PnP Modern Search web parts have duplicate trimming turned off by default, which I always recommend as the sensible setting[14].

---

[14] https://www.techmikael.com/2013/12/duplicate-trimming-in-sharepoint-2013.html

The search result item does not reflect the SharePoint item

Sometimes the metadata for an item appear different in the search results compared to in SharePoint. This can for example be differences in the title, the author or the last modified time.

Latest SharePoint version is a minor version

Search results in SharePoint Online always show values from the last major version of an item, unless *Draft Item Security* for the list or library is set to *Any user who can read item.*

If the last saved version is a minor version, that version must be published or approved if approval is enables for search to index the last changes.

This will be the case where you edit a modern page and save it as *Draft* without publishing it.

Item has not been indexed yet

In most cases an item in SharePoint is indexed within 5 minutes of the last change. However, as SharePoint Online is a cloud environment shared with many others, indexing may be queued up and can take up to as much as 24 hours before a change is reflected.

If a changed item is not discoverable in the crawl log within 24 hours, and you know everything else is correct, you should log a support ticket as described in *10 File a support ticket (page 97)*.

Troubleshooting steps

Someone reports that a certain file stored in SharePoint or a SharePoint list item is not showing in the search results.

The very first step is to check Office 365 health for any issues which could be related.

- Navigate to the Office 365 tenant admin site
- Navigate to the **Service Health** page and see if there are any incidents or advisories related to search.

If all looks good, it's time to start figuring out what the issue is.

SharePoint related messages also show on the home page of the SharePoint Admin center.

Step 1 – Acquire the item URL

To troubleshoot why a particular item is not showing you need to acquire the URL and location of the item in question, as well as know which user interface the user was searching from. The URL of the search page is the easy part, and will most likely be SharePoint Home, office.com or search from within a site or from a library.

Retrieving the URL of the actual item in question can be tricky as the modern user interface in SharePoint don't show this directly.

One way to retrieve the URL is to ask the user to use the **Copy link** feature in the library or list.

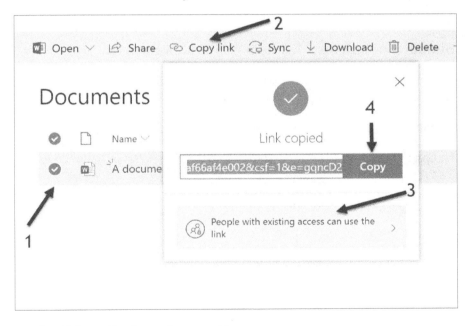

1. Select the item in question

2. Click the **Copy link** button

3. Make sure the **People with existing access can use the link** option is selected

4. Click the **Copy** button

For a document, the URL might look like:

```
https://contoso.sharepoint.com/:w:/r/teams/MyTeam/Share
d%20Documents/A%20document.docx?d=wbe79aceb386045d68583
caf66af4e002&csf=1&e=KRj1B2
```

To use this URL for troubleshooting you need to clean it up a bit. First remove the **:w:/r** bit, and secondly remove everything from the **?** and out. This leaves you with a cleaned-up URL which can be used with the crawl log and for searching.

```
https://contoso.sharepoint.com/teams/MyTeam/Shared%20Do
cuments/A%20document.docx
```

Similarly, a link for a list item might look like:

```
https://contoso.sharepoint.com/teams/MyTeam/Lists/A%20l
ist/DispForm.aspx?ID=1&e=M5v1hK
```

Cleaning it up is to remove everything after the ID=1 part.

```
https://contoso.sharepoint.com/teams/MyTeam/Lists/A%20l
ist/DispForm.aspx?ID=1
```

Armed with the URL it's time to start digging!

Step 2 – Search for the item

If you are supposed to have read access to the item in question yourself, verify that the item indeed is not showing up in search results by issuing a *path* query.

Using either PnP PowerShell, the Search Query Tool or the same UI the user was searching from, issue the following query:

```
path:"<full url of item>"
```

If you are searching for a file, you may also try:

```
documentlink:"<full url of item>"
```

as some file types are storing the list item URL in the path property instead of the full document URL.

If nothing shows, go *to Step 3 – Verify that the URL you are using is correct (page 54).*

If the item does show, try adding the search terms the user was using to locate the document.

If the item does not show with the added terms, go to *Step 10 – Check if the terms searched for are indexed (page 62).*

If the item does show using PnP PowerShell or the Search Query Tool, but not from the search UI, see *7 Query modifications (page 91).*

Step 3 – Verify that the URL you are using is correct

First verify that the item exists in the SharePoint site and then verify you are using the right URL in your property query.

Once verified and still no results, go to *Step 4 – Check the crawl log (page 54).*

Step 4 – Check the crawl log

Check the crawl log to see if the item has been indexed successfully or with errors using:

```
Get-PnPSearchCrawlLog -Filter "<full url of item>"
```

If the crawl log shows empty go to *Step 5 – Check that you have a major version (page 55).*

If you get a crawl log entry back, check the entry for errors, as well as compare the crawl log **ItemTime** with the last modified time of the item in SharePoint.

If you get an error go to *9 Interpreting crawl log errors (page 96).* If the dates differ (adjusted for time zones) go to *Step 5 – Check that you have a major version (page 55).*

Non-document files may appear as list items in the crawl log and search index, being listed with a DispForm.aspx?ID=XX URL instead of the filename.

Step 5 – Check that you have a major version

In SharePoint Online only major versions of items are indexed and made searchable by default, unless draft versions are explicitly enabled to be indexed on the list/library. This means that any draft items will not appear in your search results.

Navigate to the list or library and check the items version history.

If you have issues finding the list or library via **Site contents**, then you either don't have access or the list/library is hidden.

*The following PnP PowerShell can be used to check if a library named **Document** is hidden.*

```
Connect-PnPOnline -Url <url of the site of the item>

$library = Get-PnPList -Identity Documents

$library.Hidden
```

If the above command return true, then the library is set not to be indexed.

If you only see minor versions for the item, you need to publish at least one major version, as minor versions are not indexed for search. It might not be intentional for the list or library to use minor versions. If so, change to **only use major versions**[15].

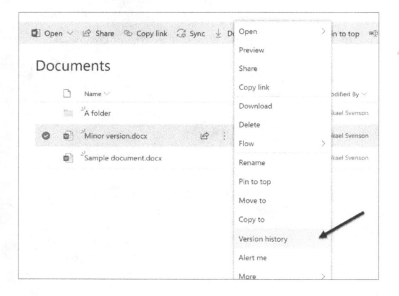

---

[15] https://support.office.com/article/enable-and-configure-versioning-for-a-list-or-library-1555d642-23ee-446a-990a-bcab618c7a37

If the last version of the item is a major version, go to *Step 6 – Check that the list/library is not blocked from indexing (page 58)*.

If the last entry is a minor version, have the user publish a major version and wait until it is indexed to ensure the original query terms used are indexed as from the document.

You can follow the direction in *Step 4 – Check the crawl log (page 54)* and retry the command until you item has been indexed (typically within 5 minutes but may take longer). Once you see the item is indexed, re-check searching from *Step 2 – Search for the item (page 53)*.

Step 6 – Check that the list/library is not blocked from indexing

- Navigate to list or library settings for where the item is stored.

- Click **Advanced settings**.

- Check that **Allow items from this document library to appear in search results?** Is set to **Yes**.

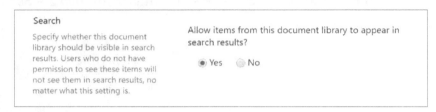

If the setting is set to yes, go to *Step 7 – Check that the site is not blocked from indexing (page 59)*.

Step 7 – Check that the site is not blocked from indexing

- Navigate to the site settings for where the item is stored.

- Navigate to **Search and offline availability**.

- Check that **Allow this site to appear in search results?** is set to **Yes**.

If the setting is set to yes, go to *10 File a support ticket (page 97)*. If not, go to *Step 8 – Verify that the user has access to the item (page 60)*.

Step 8 – Verify that the user has access to the item

First ask the user if he/she can access or open the item in question. If not, verify the access yourself. This may be done via the SharePoint UI.

- Show information for the item.
- Click **Manage access**.

- Click the **Advanced** link in the bottom right.
- Click **Check Permissions**.

- Enter the name of the user and click **Check Now** to verify that the user at least has read access.

If the user has the appropriate read permissions to the item go to *Step 9 – Re-index the list/library (page 61).*

Step 9 – Re-index the list/library

See the chapter *5 Re-index the list, library or site (page 87)* for scenarios which require re-indexing of an item. Typically only when a schema change has occurred after the items were created.

Step 10 – Check if the terms searched for are indexed

By default, the text stored in a SharePoint column is made searchable. There are however cases where a column's text is not made searchable as explained in *What makes a SharePoint column searchable? (page 32)*.

The most common case where this happens is for lists and libraries with a column named *Description*[16]. The crawled property for this column is already mapped to a managed property named *Description*, which is not searchable.

The solution for these special cases is to globally create a new managed property of type text and map the crawled properties in question to this new managed property.

I like to name mine *TotalRecall*, as a homage to the original movie as well as to explain that it will yield search recall.

---

[16] https://www.techmikael.com/2014/12/solution-to-cannot-search-content-in.html

Name and description

Name and optional description for this property.

Property name:

TotalRecall

Description:

Type

Type of information that is stored in this property.

The type of information in this property:

- ◉ Text
- ○ Integer
- ○ Decimal
- ○ Date and Time
- ○ Yes/No
- ○ Double precision float
- ○ Binary

Main characteristics

Searchable:

☑ Searchable

The caveat for a column named Description is that you need to map both the crawled property *Office:6*, and *ows_Description* to capture all scenarios. Once you have mapped the crawled properties go to *Step 9 – Re-index the list/library (page 61)*.

PROPERTY NAME	TYPE	MULTI	QUERY	SEARCH	RETRIEVE	REFINE	SORT	SAFE	MAPPED CRAWLED PROPERTIES
TotalRecall	Text	-	-	Search	-	-	-	-	Office:6, ows_Description

To check if someone has inadvertently mapped a crawled property to a non-searchable managed property you can use the PnP cmdlet **Get-PnPSearchConfiguration** *(page 19)* on the site collection in question or at the tenant level to get a list of all custom property mappings.

Crawled and managed properties issues

Examine available managed properties and crawled properties for an item

By using the SharePoint Search Query Tool you have the ability to see which retrievable managed properties are available for a specific item, as well as see what crawled properties *(v2.8.5 or newer)* are available for querying or mapping to a managed property for an item.

When you expand a result, you see two links at the end of the result.

- Managed properties

- Crawled property names

If you click on *Managed properties*, you are presented with a list similar to the image below, giving you an overview of what retrievable managed properties and values are available in search for this item.

All Properties of Item	— □ ×
Query: WorkId:"17647402104802"	

_ranking_features_	
Author	Mikael Svenson
AuthorOWSUSER	| Mikael Svenson | 693A30232E667C6D656D626572736869707C6D696B7376656E736F6E40746563686D6 96B61656C2E636F6D i:0#.f|membership|
Color	#CA5010
contentclass	STS_ListItem_GenericList
ContentDatabaseId	{d7e65bc6-7598-4bcb-8619-ef2815be63bb}
ContentExcludeFromSummaries	
ContentModifiedTime	
Contents	
ContentSource	SharePoint Content
ContentType	Item
ContentTypeId	0x0100F9973D12A979ED42B278B96800D24343
CrawledProperties	
Created	2019-11-13T09:10:32.0000000Z
CreatedBy	Mikael Svenson
CreatedById	11
CreatedOWSDATE	2019-11-13T09:10:32Z
Culture	nb-NO
DefaultEncodingURL	/TestTeam/Lists/A%20list/13_.000
DepartmentId	{35a48fd1-f757-4ff4-9d30-4cf574305616}
DetectedLanguage	en
DetectedLanguageRanking	9
DiscoveredTime	2019-11-13T09:12:49.2896794Z
DisplayAuthor	Mikael Svenson

Clicking *Crawled property names* lists crawled properties available for the item itself. You will not see the actual values of the crawled properties, but the list can help troubleshoot if you have mapped the correct crawled property or not for a column.

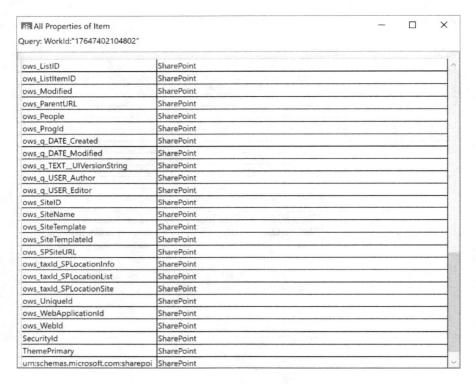

All Properties of Item	— □ ×
Query: WorkId:"17647402104802"	
ows_ListID	SharePoint
ows_ListItemID	SharePoint
ows_Modified	SharePoint
ows_ParentURL	SharePoint
ows_People	SharePoint
ows_ProgId	SharePoint
ows_q_DATE_Created	SharePoint
ows_q_DATE_Modified	SharePoint
ows_q_TEXT__UIVersionString	SharePoint
ows_q_USER_Author	SharePoint
ows_q_USER_Editor	SharePoint
ows_SiteID	SharePoint
ows_SiteName	SharePoint
ows_SiteTemplate	SharePoint
ows_SiteTemplateId	SharePoint
ows_SPSiteURL	SharePoint
ows_taxId_SPLocationInfo	SharePoint
ows_taxId_SPLocationList	SharePoint
ows_taxId_SPLocationSite	SharePoint
ows_UniqueId	SharePoint
ows_WebApplicationId	SharePoint
ows_WebId	SharePoint
SecurityId	SharePoint
ThemePrimary	SharePoint
urn:schemas.microsoft.com:sharepoi	SharePoint

In order access the available managed and crawled properties names lists, query for refiner values for the two special refinable managed properties:

- ManagedProperties
- CrawledProperties

Crawled properties not appearing for site columns

For a crawled property to be created for a SharePoint column you must have at least one item with a value in the column. A crawled property should appear when the following steps have been taken:

1. Add or create a column for a list or library.
2. Create a new item or modify an existing one and ensure there is a value in the column added.
3. Ensure the item is a major version.
4. Wait for the item to appear in search.

If for some reason the item does appear in search, but the crawled property is missing, try the following work-around.

1. Navigate to
   `https://<tenant>.sharepoint.com/sites/yoursite/_layouts/15/user.aspx`
2. Manually add your user account with full permissions to the site collection.
3. Request a re-index of the site (see *Re-indexing a list or library* on page 88).
4. Once the items are re-index, which is easiest to test by adding a new item and checking for the item to appear in search, then the crawled property should be present.

Managed property does not contain a value even though I mapped it to a crawled property

Crawled and managed properties are somewhat like the chicken and the egg. You first need to create an item, and have it indexed for the crawled property to appear in the search schema. Next you need to map the crawled property to a managed property if you want to query or refine on the data. Once mapped, you need to re-index all items for the managed property to be populated.

If you have correctly mapped a crawled property to a managed property, and the managed property appear empty, perform the steps in *Re-indexing a list or library (page 87)* and once the item is re-crawled, data should appear as long as the managed property is set to be retrievable.

Automatic crawled and managed properties are missing

In SharePoint when you create a list column, this column will by default result in two crawled properties and one managed property as explained in *Automatically created managed properties (page 24)*.

However, if you have previously created a list or site column with the same name, new properties will not be created for you as SharePoint sees that you already have a crawled property matching the column.

To exemplify: If a user created a column named *Color* on some library, a corresponding crawled property *ows_Color* will be made available to search. If you later create a new site column with the same name Color of type choice, and expect to see the automatic managed property *ColorOWSCHCS*, it will not be there.

As a rule, when creating site columns used for search is to check if there is a crawled or managed property available already for the name to avoid any conflicts.

Or even better, **always prefix** your columns with something unique, to ensure unique crawled and property names.

Crawled and managed properties for user profiles

A common issue seen with people search surfaces when you have custom user profile properties which you want to make searchable. Say you add a new user profile property named *FavoriteColor*. When someone queries for the term *red*, you want all profiles matching this term returned.

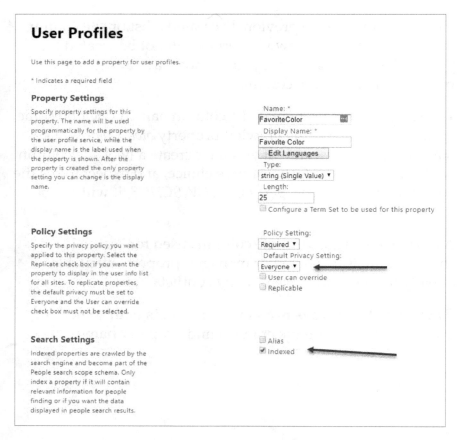

First of all, the property should be set to be available to *Everyone*, and secondly it should be set to be *Indexed*, to ensure a crawled property is created for the value.

If you read *What makes a SharePoint column searchable? (page 32)*, you see that for SharePoint content the value stored in a crawled property is searchable in the full-text index. This is also true for crawled properties coming from user profiles, however, the value is stored in the *Default* full-text index, not the *PeopleIdx* full-text index which is needed for user profile search.

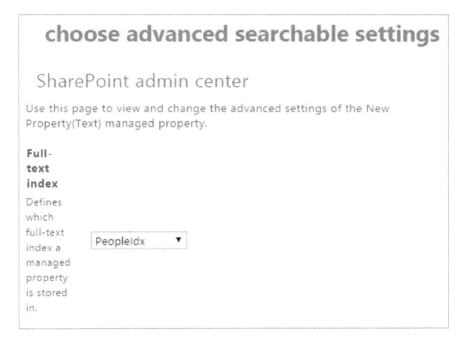

In order to solve this and get recall for values in an index profile property you have to map the crawled property to a managed property marked as *searchable*, and which has the full-text index set to *PeopleIdx*. Taking the *FavoriteColor* profile property as an example you map the crawled property *People:Favorite* to the managed property *ContentsHidden*. ContentsHidden is an out of the box managed property which already contains a lot of the other profile properties, thus made for this exact purpose.

If you also need to do property queries and want to retrieve the value from a custom user profile property, then map the crawled property to a RefinableStringXX property as well.

Do not change the full-text index of the RefinableStringXX properties as they are re-used for other content as well. For user profile properties it is better to map the crawled property twice, once to a property having the PeopleIdx full-text index for recall, and once for property queries, refiners and retrieval.

Once you have completed mapping the crawled property corresponding to user profile property, you need to re-index all the user profiles to ensure the values are set correct in the index.

See *6 Re-index user profiles (page 89)* for how to re-index user profiles.

Tokenization of managed properties

Tokenization or the handling of characters in regard to casing, diacritics and special characters are important in search. Typically, you want a query for *contoso marketing* to also match *contoso-marketing* or *cøntosö-markéting*. The default behavior by SharePoint Online search is to tokenize based on the detected language. There are cases where this might not work as intended, and you may instead use one of the following settings:

- **Language Neutral Tokenization** – useful if you have multilingual content stored in the managed property.
- Finer Query Tokenization – useful if you have special characters stored in the managed property, such as identifiers (1-12-456#7) that you want to query for.

Complete matching on managed properties

If you build business applications on top of search you sometimes want to retrieve items by the exact value in a specific field. If this value contains spaces or special characters, you may check the **Complete Matching** setting for a custom managed property. If the property contains values such as *ID-1234-1234*, you will only get a match if you search for this exact value, and not for any other value, including the use of wildcards.

If you search for *ID-1234-**, you will not get a match on the above example, as the * character will be treated as the character * itself and not as a wild card representation otherwise used in KQL. To do partial matches on these kinds of content look at using *Finer Query Tokenization*.

Complete Matching:
By default, search returns partial
matches between queries against this
managed property and its content.
Select Complete Matching for search
to return exact matches instead. If a
managed property "Title" contains
"Contoso Sites", only the query Title:
"Contoso Sites" will give a result.

Your change takes effect after you've
crawled the relevant content.

☑ Complete Matching

Alias usage on managed properties

Ever since SharePoint 2013 shipped SharePoint search has
supported the use of alias names for managed properties. The
typical use case being you have a custom column in a
SharePoint library which you want to use in search as a filter
or refiner. You map the crawled property for your column
ows_MyColumn to for example *RefinableString100* and give it
an alias explaining the content, say *DocumentStatus*. This
allows you to craft queries like *DocumentStatus:draft* instead of
RefinableString100:draft. More readable and more descriptive.

*You may add multiple aliases to a managed
property by separating the aliases with a
semicolon.*

So far, so good. What happens if you name your alias the same name as an existing managed property like *Title* or *LastModifiedTime*? It had never occurred to me this was possible, but what happens is that your aliases take precedence and you have effectively taken over the values for those properties.

The left version in the above image shows the original values while the right shows the crawl date string for the title and last modified date via an alias on *RefinableString100*.

PROPERTY NAME	TYPE	MULTI	QUERY	SEARCH	RETRIEVE	REFINE	SORT	SAFE	MAPPED CRAWLED PROPERTIES	ALIASES
RefinableString100	Text	Multi	Query		Retrieve	Refine	Sort	Safe	Internal:323	PzlCrawlTime, Title, LastModifiedTime

As you can imagine Microsoft Search and the built-in search experiences takes a dependency on what values to expect for many of the out of the box managed properties. Which means you need to take care when you use aliases to ensure you're not using a name already in use.

The good thing is that the fix is easy – remove the aliases and it all goes back to normal.

Breaking search by mapping more crawled properties to existing managed properties

Take a managed property such as *SPSiteUrl*. The default configuration is to populate it with the value from *ows_SPSiteURL*, the site collection URL for an item.

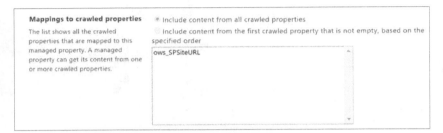

There is nothing stopping you from adding more crawled properties to this list, but the option to only use the first and not all values is disabled. The result could end up with the managed property containing multiple values instead of the expected singular value – something built-in search UI's might not have considered. Because why should you?

The fix is still easy, remove your added crawled property mapping and re-index the content.

Searching against managed metadata

One of the great features in SharePoint is ability to define taxonomies via the term store and use these taxonomies as columns in SharePoint lists and libraries as well as for user profile property values.

A feature of the term store is that a term can have both synonyms as well as language translated labels. When this feature is being used it allows users of different languages to see pick and view the terms in their native language.

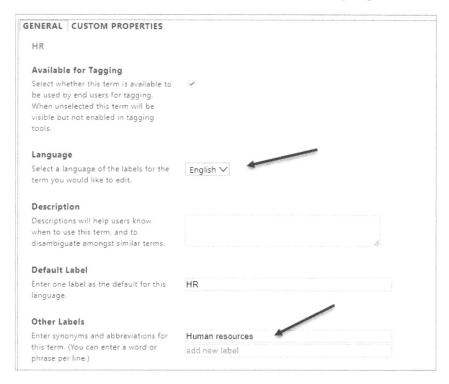

The caveat when it comes to search is that only the default label in the default language is being indexed. For the above term *HR*, you would only get recall on that term and not for *human resources*, or any other language translations.

Currently there is no easy fix for this when it comes to the Microsoft Search result pages outside of building your own synonym expansion logic in a custom search page.

For classic search you can take a look at the open source project **https://github.com/SPCSR/HelperFunctions/blob/master/SPO-Search-Improvements/readme.md** which has synonym expansion capabilities.

For modern search experiences within SharePoint, you will be able to use a special type of SharePoint Framework Extension which can modify the original issued query, or build upon or use the existing synonym capabilities of the PnP Modern Search web parts[17].

---

[17] https://github.com/microsoft-search/pnp-modern-search

Impact of query language in search

When a search query is being issued the returned result or recall will be better if search knows the language of the query and the content you are targeting.

The reason being that by knowing the query language search can use language features such as including plural forms or multiple forms of diacritics when returning the result. As a simple example, searching for *car*, also returns results for *cars*, when issuing the query in English.

By default, the search UIs in SharePoint will use the user's user interface language, or browser language to detect the language being used. In classic search a user can override this by picking a language, while in modern search this is not possible.

In order to get the best search result possible, it is recommended to align the user interface language for Office 365 and SharePoint Online with most of the content. For businesses that have content in multiple languages, expect the search offerings in Office 365 to solve these issues going forward, using smarter approaches to detect the intent and language of a search query.

Duplicate instances of refiner values

Every so often there is a question on refiner values that when looking at it in the UI you see something like the image below.

By the looks of it something went wrong with search and *Sales* appears twice as a refiner value. While it looks to be an error, the error is in the data source where one of the values contains one or more spaces before or after the actual term.

If the data comes from a term set, ensure you don't have two terms, one with a space and one without. If the data being synchronized comes from a line of business system, ensure data is normalized and space trimmed when synchronizing it to avoid these kinds of issues.

Similar issues can happen if the value contains ampersand &, which can also represent as & visually very similar, but a different Unicode character (\uFF06).

Why does one item appear above another in the search results?

Explaining or troubleshooting this is very hard. Most times we don't have any insights into how the rank models for SharePoint Online are built or work and they will also adapt over time depending on content and user behavior via machine learning models.

That said, there are some basic principles which comes into play.

- Term matches in for example the Title field of an item counts more than the body text of a document. Ranking of fields is using a BM25F model[18], where individual fields have been given different weights. The SharePoint 2013 documentation[18] on rank model gives some insights into properties being ranked, and how much, but these weights are constantly changed by Microsoft ensuring the best ranking possible.
- In rank models using personalization context, content produced by someone you work with, as related via the Microsoft Graph, will have higher relevance than other content.
- Newer or fresher content has higher relevance compared to older content.
- Content used and viewed more compared to other content has a higher relevance.

---

[18] https://docs.microsoft.com/en-us/sharepoint/dev/general-development/customizing-ranking-models-to-improve-relevance-in-sharepoint#bm25

Due to these factors, relevance will change over time, and doing a deep analysis and comparison is hard as rank scores are also normalized.

The SharePoint Search Query Tool have an option you can use to try deciphering the rank score of a search result. Check the **Include Rank Detail** checkbox, which will provide a link per item **Show rank details….**

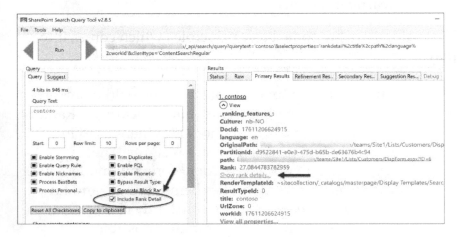

You need to have the SharePoint Admin role or be a Global Admin in order to see rank details.

Clicking the link will open a window with rank details for the item. In the image below you see the term *Contoso* matching in the Title property and body contents for an item – each contributing a different part of the rank score.

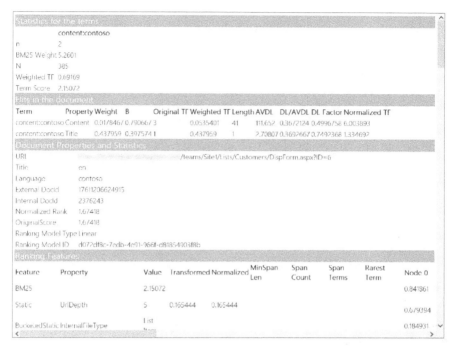

The property *Title* being listed does not necessarily mean the Title property itself. It could also be a managed property where the weight group has been changed to the same context level as the Title managed property (level 1).

This setting is available on a managed properties *Advanced Searchable Settings* page.

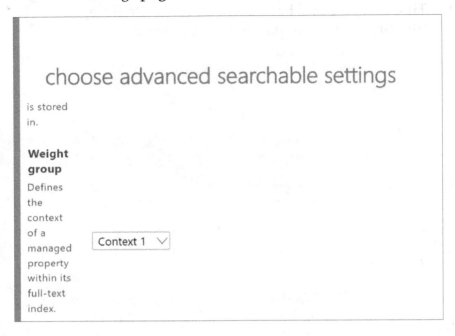

Context 1 does not necessarily mean more important than *Context 14*. To know which context contributes the most to an item rank you need to know how properties are actually configured in the rank model being used – information not available in SharePoint Online.

To sum it up, explaining rank is hard, and you should think that the most important item will appear on top of the result, and Microsoft is constantly working to improve search relevance making users more efficient in their daily job.

API issues causing partial results being returned

Private Office 365 Groups

In some cases, results from private groups are not being returned. By adding EnableDynamicGroups set to true, all results should appear.

In a REST GET query append the following to include results from private groups.

```
&properties='EnableDynamicGroups:true'
```

Multi-geo tenants

If your Office 365 tenant spans over multiple geographic locations, you need to add a special parameter in order to aggregate results from the search index corresponding to each geographic location.

In a REST GET query append the following to include results from all geographic locations.

```
&properties='EnableMultiGeoSearch:true'
```

OneDrive items

By default, OneDrive items are no longer being returned together with other SharePoint items when using the search API.

It is possible to have OneDrive items returned. The user will see a secondary result set in the returned search results.

In a REST GET query append the following to include results from OneDrive sites.

```
&properties='ContentSetting:3'
```

See the official documentation[19] for more information regarding this parameter.

---

[19] https://docs.microsoft.com/sharepoint/dev/general-development/sharepoint-search-rest-api-overview#contentsetting

5 Re-index the list, library or site

In most cases an item in SharePoint is indexed or crawled within 5 minutes after the last modification done. Usually the only reason when you need to trigger re-indexing manually for items is when you have changed crawled to managed property mappings which relates to content already being indexed. For these cases re-indexing is needed to ensure the population of data in the managed properties occurs.

Re-indexing a list or library

To mark a list or library for re-indexing perform the following steps.

- Go to **List/Library settings**.

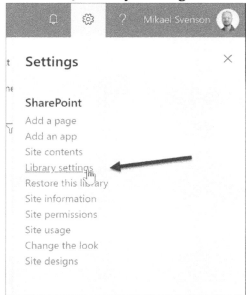

- Click **Advanced settings**.

- Scroll down and click the re-index button, as well as the button in the dialog which opens.

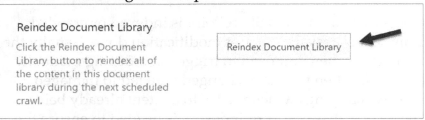

Reindex Document Library

Click the Reindex Document Library button to reindex all of the content in this document library during the next scheduled crawl.

Reindex Document Library

- Wait until re-index has happened by checking the crawl log or search for the item until you see it is updated.

6 Re-index user profiles

While SharePoint content is being picked up and re-indexed quite frequently after a modification to the security for the item, or to the item itself, this is not the case for user profiles.

User profiles are indexed on a schedule and typically will be visible within 6 hours of a change to a profile, but you should wait up until a whole day before being concerned. Working with search and user profiles in SharePoint Online requires patience and there is no way around it unless you hit the crawl schedule right on.

As with other content, the only scenario requiring a re-index of user profiles is when you change crawled to managed property mappings for content already being indexed.

To trigger re-indexing of a user profile you need to cause an update on the user profile itself, to change the last modified date. You want to do this without changing the profile itself.

At **https://github.com/wobba/SPO-Trigger-Reindex**[20] you will find a script which iterates all user profiles to cause an update in the profile.

---

[20] https://github.com/wobba/SPO-Trigger-Reindex

A quicker approach if you have many user profiles is to use the bulk update API for SharePoint[21]. Check out the PnP PowerShell cmdlet **New-PnPUPABulkImportJob**[22] on how to do this via PowerShell. The flow would be to generate a file with all users and for example set the *Department* value to the same value already stored for the user. Once the bulk import is complete, the user profiles will have an updated last modified time stamp and will be picked up by the next user profile crawl.

---

[21] https://docs.microsoft.com/sharepoint/dev/solution-guidance/bulk-user-profile-update-api-for-sharepoint-online

[22] https://docs.microsoft.com/powershell/module/sharepoint-pnp/new-pnpupabulkimportjob

7 Query modifications

One of the most common reasons for a search query to not return results as expected is because the query has been re-written.

For classic search this can happen inside the query template of a webpart. For other scenarios it can happen due to a query rule intercepting the query or that the default search result source in the scope you are searching from has been changed.

Check if a query was modified

When a query is issued to SharePoint it may be modified by the query template on the query itself, by the result source being used, or by a query rule.

A somewhat common scenario is to modify the default result source on either the tenant level or site collection level to exclude certain types of content[23].

Below I have created a custom result source which is set as the default on a site collection.

---

[23] https://www.techmikael.com/2015/03/how-to-unexpectedly-block-usage-of.html

If the query template is modified to only return docx files by appending *filetype:docx* to the query template, then all searches performed on the site or in lists and libraries will have the filter applied. This means document libraries will only yield matches for Word documents while lists won't return any items at all.

To check if the default result source has been modified, navigate to the Search Result Sources page for the tenant (via the SharePoint search admin center), the site collection or a site, and see if a there is a custom result source set as default, and if it employs any filters which may impact searches.

The default result source in SharePoint Online without any modification is named *Local SharePoint Results*, and is using the following query template:

```
{?{searchTerms} -ContentClass=urn:content-class:SPSPeople}
```

Browser debug

Before issuing the query from SharePoint press F12 in your browser to open dev tools. Next navigate to the network tab, and filter out search queries by filtering on:

`_api/search`

Copy the JSON output from the response window and find the modification.

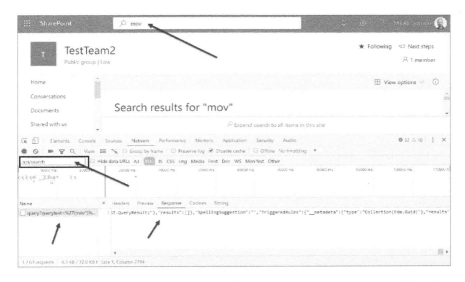

Nicely formatted for the sample above you can see the final query being executed, where filters have been added to scope the query to one library only.

```
}, {
    "Key": "QueryModification",
    "Value": "(mov*) siteid:{b0508a92-4d48-4519-9d77-5c020ac556a8}
    (webid:{c940a817-8ad2-49a6-b9a2-e396524d2006} OR webid:c940a817-8ad2-49e6-b9a2-e396524d2006) path:\"
    https:/           sharepoint.com/teams/TestTeam2/Pics\" ContentTypeId:0x0*
    -ContentClass-urn:content-class:SPSPeople",
    "ValueType": "Edm.String"
```

SharePoint Search Query Tool debugging

Similarly using the SharePoint Query Tool, you can see any re-writes in the Status tab as well as if any query rules were applied.

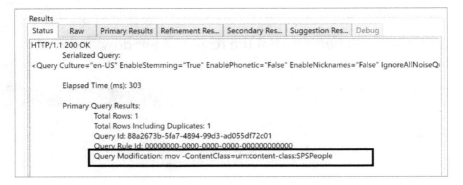

8 External users and search

In general, external users can search any content they have access to either directly or via any security group they are a member of. They are however not members of any of the default *Everyone* security groups, unless a tenant admin has explicitly changed this behavior.

When content or a site is made accessible to an external user, you must wait for a security crawl to be run before the content is searchable. This should not take very long. However, if you experience content not being searchable for external users you may try to trigger re-indexing of the content as explained in *5 Re-index the list, library or site (page 87)*.

If you employ custom solutions via the SharePoint Framework (SPFx) which provide search solutions, you must ensure the external users can load the solution from the Application catalog. You either must grant them permission to the app catalog site or enable the SharePoint Online public CDN feature[24].

---

[24] https://docs.microsoft.com/office365/enterprise/use-office-365-cdn-with-spo

9 Interpreting crawl log errors

Parser: Document was partially processed. The parser was not able to parse the entire document.

The error *Parser: Document was partially processed. The parser was not able to parse the entire document.* can appear if:

- The document is password protected
- The document is AIP protected and encrypted
- The file is larger than the supported file size for indexing. See **Search limits for SharePoint Online**[25] for supported limits.

Parser: Max output size of 2000000 has been reached while parsing!

The error *Parser: Max output size of 2,000,000 has been reached while parsing!* can appear for long documents which has more than 2 million characters in them. The content before the character limit is indexed and searchable, while content after is not.

---

[25] https://docs.microsoft.com/sharepoint/search-limits

10 File a support ticket

If all avenues have been exhausted, write up all your troubleshooting steps and file a support ticket with Microsoft to help resolve your issue. You can do this by going to https://admin.microsoft.com and clicking on the Support menu in the left hand navigation. If you have a premiere support agreement with Microsoft, consider using this avenue as well.

11 Community information

Another useful avenue for enlisting help is the SharePoint and search community at large. The below communities and web sites are likely places to get help if you ask in thoughtful manner :)

- Tech and Me – Author's blog
  https://www.techmikael.com

- Microsoft Tech Community – SharePoint
  https://techcommunity.microsoft.com/t5/SharePoint/bd-p/SharePoint_General

- SharePoint on Stack Exchange
  https://sharepoint.stackexchange.com/

- Microsoft Search UserVoice
  https://office365.uservoice.com/forums/925270-microsoft-search

- SharePoint Search UserVoice
  https://sharepoint.uservoice.com/forums/330321-sharepoint-search

- Search Explained Yammer Community
  https://www.yammer.com/searchexplained

- Search Explained YouTube videos
  https://youtube.com/searchexplained

- AbleBlue YouTube videos
  https://www.youtube.com/ableblue